ML DEMYSTIFIED: UNLOCKING THE POWER OF MACHINE LEARNING WITHOUT THE JARGON

A Comprehensive Guide for Non-Technicians and Technicians

By Ivan Kuznietsov

I

COPYRIGHT AND DISCLAIMERS

Legal Disclaimer:

The views expressed in this book are solely those of the author and do not necessarily reflect the views of any organization the author is affiliated with. The author makes no representations as to the accuracy or completeness of any information provided in this book.

DEDICATION

To my family, who has always believed in my dreams and supported me on this incredible writing journey.

EPIGRAPH

"Imagination is more important than knowledge. For knowledge is limited, whereas imagination embraces the entire world, stimulating progress, giving birth to evolution." - Albert Einstein

ABOUT THE AUTHOR

Hi, my name is Ivan Kuznietsov. I was born in Ukraine and my professional journey has taken me across diverse industries throughout Europe, bestowing me with invaluable insights and experiences along the way. I am a certified Scrum Master and Agile Coach with a deep passion for the world of artificial intelligence (AI). As an avid learner and practitioner in the field of AI, I combine my expertise in Agile methodologies with my enthusiasm for artificial intelligence, using a storytelling approach to demystify complex concepts and make them accessible to readers of all backgrounds.

ABOUT THE BOOK SERIES

This book is a part of *the "AI from A to Z: Decoding Artificial Intelligence for Non-Technicians and Technicians"* series which is a comprehensive guide that takes you on a step-by-step journey through the world of AI. From the basics to advanced topics, each book in the series unravels the complexities of AI and presents them clearly and concisely. Whether you're new to AI or looking to expand your knowledge, this series is your go-to resource for understanding and leveraging the power of AI.

ABOUT THE BOOK

"ML Demystified: Unlocking the Power of Machine Learning without the Jargon" is a comprehensive guide that makes machine learning accessible to everyone. Whether you're a non-technician or a technician, this book empowers you to explore the world of machine learning with confidence. Through engaging storytelling and real-life examples, we demystify complex concepts, introduce different types of ML algorithms, and unveil the power of predictive modeling and pattern recognition. With no prior technical expertise required, this guide equips you with the knowledge and tools to harness the transformative potential of machine learning.

PREFACE

Welcome to the world of "ML Demystified: Unlocking the Power of Machine Learning without the Jargon." In this concise yet comprehensive preface, I invite you to embark on a remarkable journey into the realm of machine learning. Whether you are a non-technician or a technician, this guide offers an accessible and engaging approach to demystify the complexities of machine learning. With real-life examples and simplified explanations, I aim to empower you with the knowledge and understanding needed to navigate this exciting field. Get ready to unlock the power of machine learning and embark on a transformative adventure. Let's begin!

CONTENTS

INTRODUCTION

"The question of whether a computer can think is no more interesting than the question of whether a submarine can swim." - Edsger Dijkstra

In the vast expanse of human history, few advancements have captured our collective imagination and sparked as much curiosity as the realm of artificial intelligence (AI) and its most transformative discipline: machine learning (ML). From science fiction novels to blockbuster movies, the concept of machines that can learn and make intelligent decisions has tantalized our minds and fueled our dreams of a future where the boundaries between humans and machine blur.

Today, we stand at the cusp of a technological revolution, where machine learning is reshaping industries, revolutionizing the way we live and work, and offering unprecedented possibilities for innovation. It is no longer confined to the realms of science fiction. Machine learning has become an integral part of our reality, influencing everything from the products we use to the services we rely on.

But what exactly is machine learning? How does it work? And why is it considered the driving force behind the AI revolution? In this book, we embark on a captivating journey into the world of machine learning, demystifying its concepts, unraveling its applications, and exploring the profound impact it has on our lives.

At its core, machine learning is the art and science of enabling computers to learn from data and make informed decisions without being explicitly programmed. It is about creating algorithms and models that can analyze vast amounts of information, recognize patterns, and extract meaningful insights to guide future actions. By leveraging the power of data, machine learning empowers us to tackle complex problems, unlock hidden knowledge, and make predictions with remarkable accuracy.

As we delve into the intricacies of machine learning, we will witness the incredible power of algorithms that can predict the weather, recommend personalized content, diagnose diseases, drive autonomous vehicles, and even compose music. We will unravel the mysteries of deep learning, reinforcement learning, and unsupervised learning, understanding their unique capabilities and real-world applications.

But this journey is not solely about technicalities and algorithms. It is about the profound impact machine learning has on our lives, society, and the very essence of what it means to be human. We will explore the ethical considerations surrounding machine learning, discussing topics such as bias, privacy, transparency, and accountability. We will delve into the potential societal implications, contemplating the future of work, education, healthcare, and the nature of human creativity and innovation in a world increasingly influenced by intelligent machines.

Throughout this book, we will navigate the vast landscape of machine learning with a sense of wonder and curiosity, embracing the stories and examples that bring the concepts to life. We will demystify the jargon and technicalities, making the subject accessible to both non-technicians and technicians alike. Each chapter will take you on a journey, exploring the intricacies of different aspects of machine learning while highlighting their practical applications and real-world impact.

As we embark on this adventure together, I hope that you will not only gain a deep understanding of machine learning but also develop a sense of awe and appreciation for the possibilities it presents. Whether you are a seasoned professional seeking to expand your knowledge or a curious individual eager to explore the frontiers of technology, this book will be your guide, providing insights, inspiration, and a roadmap to navigate the fascinating world of machine learning.

In the words of Edsger Dijkstra, let us remember that the question of whether a computer can think is no more interesting than the question of whether a submarine can swim. Machine learning has given rise to a new era of intelligence, where the boundaries of what is possible continue to expand. So, let us dive into this ocean of knowledge, explore its depths, and unveil the power of machine learning together.

***

CHAPTER 1: THE AI AWAKENING: JOURNEY INTO THE WORLD OF MACHINE LEARNING

"Artificial intelligence is the new
electricity." - Andrew Ng

As I sat in front of my computer, pondering the vast potential of technology, these words echoed in my mind. Little did I know that I was about to embark on an extraordinary journey into the world of machine learning, a journey that would forever change the way I perceived the power of artificial intelligence.

It all began on an ordinary day, much like any other. I found myself intrigued by the notion of machines that could learn and make intelligent decisions, just like humans. The concept seemed like something out of a science fiction novel, but little did I know that it was already transforming industries and reshaping our lives in ways unimaginable.

I delved into the history of AI, tracing its roots back to the pioneering work of Alan Turing and his vision of machines that could exhibit intelligent behavior. But it wasn't until the advent of machine learning that AI truly began to take shape.

Machine learning, as I soon discovered, is the art of teaching machines to learn from data and improve their performance over time. It's like unlocking the hidden potential of a dormant mind, enabling computers to analyze vast amounts of information and make informed decisions without explicit programming.

To truly grasp the power of machine learning, I needed to understand its core principles. I immersed myself in the world of algorithms, from the simplicity of linear regression to the complexity of neural networks. Each algorithm was like a brushstroke on a canvas, contributing to the masterpiece that is machine learning.

But it wasn't just about the algorithms. It was about the data. I learned that data is the lifeblood of machine learning, fueling its ability to uncover patterns, make predictions, and drive innovation. Every byte of data holds the potential to unlock new insights and revolutionize industries.

To bring the concept of machine learning to life, I thought back to a personal experience. I recalled how a recommendation algorithm on my favorite streaming platform had introduced me to a new TV series that quickly became an obsession. It was as if the algorithm had understood my preferences better than I understood myself, using patterns in my viewing history to suggest the perfect show.

The more I delved into the world of machine learning, the more I realized its vast applications. From healthcare to finance, from autonomous vehicles to personalized marketing, machine learning was permeating every aspect of our lives. It was transforming industries, solving complex problems, and paving the way for a future that was once confined to the realms of science fiction.

As I concluded my journey into the world of

machine learning, I couldn't help but feel a sense of awe and wonder. The AI awakening had shown me that the potential of technology knows no bounds. It has the power to revolutionize our world, shape the future, and unlock new frontiers of human achievement.

And so, dear reader, I invite you to join me on this incredible journey into the world of machine learning. Together, let us unravel the mysteries, embrace the possibilities, and embark on a quest to unlock the true potential of artificial intelligence. The AI awakening awaits, and the future is ours to shape.

Remember, we make just a glimpse into the captivating world of machine learning, and there is so much more to explore. So fasten your seatbelt and get ready for an adventure like no other. The journey awaits, and the possibilities are endless. Let's dive into the realm of machine learning and discover the power of AI together.

***

CHAPTER 2: THE CURIOUS CASE OF INTELLIGENT MACHINES: HOW ML IS CHANGING OUR LIVES

"Machine learning is the power
tool of the 21st century."

Have you ever stopped to wonder about the incredible machines that surround us, capable of learning, adapting, and even making decisions? These intelligent machines, driven by the magic of machine learning, are shaping our lives in ways we couldn't have imagined just a few decades ago.

Imagine a sunny afternoon when you first

witnessed the truly profound impact of machine learning on our everyday lives. As you strolled through the city streets, you found yourself captivated by the autonomous vehicles effortlessly navigating the roads. It was as if the cars had a mind of their own, using sophisticated algorithms and sensors to analyze the environment and make split-second decisions to ensure our safety.

But the influence of machine learning extended far beyond the realm of transportation. It was present in our homes, making our lives more convenient and efficient. I reminisced about the voice-activated assistant that resided in my living room, always ready to answer questions, play my favorite music, or even control the lights with a simple command. It was like having a personal AI-powered companion, constantly learning and adapting to my needs.

As I delved deeper into the world of machine learning, I discovered its impact on healthcare. The ability of intelligent machines to analyze vast amounts of medical data and assist in diagnosis was nothing short of remarkable. Soon we will hear a lot of stories about receiving a life-saving diagnosis thanks to the early detection capabilities of a machine learning system. It will be a testament to the potential of these intelligent machines to revolutionize healthcare and save countless lives.

But it wasn't just the life-altering applications of machine learning that fascinated me. It was also the smaller, yet significant, ways in which it influenced our daily routines. From personalized movie recommendations that anticipated our tastes to virtual assistants that could understand and respond to natural language, machine learning was making our lives more enjoyable and efficient.

Consider the wonders of online shopping, where machine learning algorithms analyze our browsing and purchasing patterns to offer tailored recommendations. It's like having a personal shopper who knows our preferences better than we know ourselves, leading us to discover new products and experiences we may have never encountered otherwise.

The more I immersed myself in the curious case of intelligent machines, the more I realized the immense potential they held. Machine learning had the power to transform industries, create new opportunities, and tackle some of society's most pressing challenges. It was a force driving innovation and pushing the boundaries of human achievement.

However, as with any powerful tool, machine learning also brought forth questions and concerns. The ethical implications of algorithms making decisions that affect our lives, the potential biases embedded in the data they learn from, and the need for transparency and accountability were pressing issues that required our attention. It was crucial to ensure that the development and deployment of intelligent machines were guided by a strong moral compass and a commitment to the well-being of humanity.

As I concluded my exploration of the curious case of intelligent machines, I couldn't help but feel a sense of awe and excitement for what the future holds. The impact of machine learning on our lives will only continue to grow, shaping industries, revolutionizing healthcare, and transforming the way we interact with technology.

Let's embrace this journey of discovery together. Let us marvel at the wonders of intelligent machines, while also recognizing our responsibility to navigate the ethical and societal implications they bring. The curious case of machine learning is unfolding before our eyes, and we have the opportunity to be active participants in this ever-evolving story.

The journey promises to be enlightening, exhilarating, and filled with revelations that will forever change the way we perceive the world around us.

***

CHAPTER 3: THE MAGIC INGREDIENT: UNDERSTANDING THE CORE PRINCIPLES OF MACHINE LEARNING

"Machine learning is the key that unlocks the door to the future."

Imagine a world where computers can learn and improve from experience, just like we humans do. A world where they can make accurate predictions, recognize patterns and make informed decisions without explicit programming. This is the realm of machine learning, the magic ingredient that has transformed our technological landscape.

As I delved into the fascinating world of machine learning, I found myself captivated by its core principles. It was like unraveling the secrets of a mystical recipe, discovering the ingredients that give machine learning its power and potency.

At the heart of machine learning lies the concept of data. It is the fuel that feeds the learning algorithms, enabling machines to uncover patterns and make predictions. I recalled a time when I was searching for a specific audiobook online. Little did I know that my search history, along with countless other data points, was being collected and analyzed to create a personalized recommendation system. It was this amalgamation of data that allowed the system to understand my preferences and suggest audiobooks tailored to my taste.

But data alone is not enough. Like a chef with a pantry full of ingredients, machine learning requires algorithms to transform raw data into meaningful insights. These algorithms act as the guiding recipes, instructing the machine on how to process and analyze the data. I thought back to the time when I first encountered the concept of a decision tree algorithm. It was like a flowchart, guiding the machine to make a series of decisions based on the characteristics of the data. It was through these algorithms that machines could learn and adapt, continually improving their performance.

One crucial aspect of machine learning is the **training process**. Similar to how we humans learn through experience, machines need to be exposed to vast amounts of data to develop their skills. I reminisced about a time when I discovered an image recognition system being trained. It was shown thousands of images, each labeled with the object it contained. Through this iterative process, the machine learned to recognize various objects with remarkable accuracy. It was a testament to the power of training and the immense potential of machine learning to revolutionize fields such as computer vision and natural language processing.

As I explored further, I discovered that evaluation and validation were essential components of the machine learning journey. It was not enough for a machine learning model to perform well during training. It needed to demonstrate its effectiveness on unseen data. I thought about the concept of cross-validation, where the model is tested on different subsets of the data to ensure its robustness and generalizability. This rigorous evaluation process helped ensure that the machine learning model could perform accurately in real-world scenarios.

While the core principles of machine learning may sound complex, their application can be found in various aspects of our lives. From personalized movie recommendations to virtual assistants that understand our commands, machine learning has seamlessly integrated into our daily routines. It's like having a personal assistant who knows us intimately, adapting to our preferences, and making our lives more convenient.

But with great power comes great responsibility. As machine learning continues to advance, ethical considerations become paramount. I reflected on the importance of fairness, transparency, and accountability in the development and deployment of machine learning systems. It was essential to ensure that these systems were free from biases, treated all individuals fairly, and upheld ethical standards.

As I concluded my exploration of the core principles of machine learning, I couldn't help but feel a sense of awe and wonder. Machine learning was the magic ingredient that has revolutionized the way we interact with technology, opening doors to unimaginable possibilities. Using machine learning, we can navigate this fascinating landscape, understanding its core principles and leveraging its capabilities to shape a brighter future.

***

CHAPTER 4: THE ALCHEMIST'S APPRENTICE: EXPLORING DIFFERENT TYPES OF ML ALGORITHMS

"Algorithms are the alchemist's tools that turn data into valuable insights."

As I continued my journey through the realm of machine learning, I couldn't help but be reminded of an ancient tale about an apprentice to a renowned alchemist. The apprentice, eager to learn the secrets of the alchemical arts, was introduced to a vast array of tools and techniques, each designed to transform ordinary substances into extraordinary creations.

In a similar vein, machine learning algorithms act as the alchemist's tools, enabling us to extract knowledge and meaning from raw data.

Just as the apprentice was taught to differentiate between various potions and concoctions, understanding the different types of machine learning algorithms is essential for unlocking their true potential. Each algorithm possesses unique characteristics and capabilities, making them suitable for specific tasks and datasets.

One of the most commonly encountered types of machine learning algorithms is the supervised learning algorithm. It reminded me of the apprentice's training in following strict instructions to create precise mixtures.

In **supervised learning**, the algorithms are provided with labeled training data, where the desired outputs or target variables are known. The algorithms then learn from these examples to make predictions or classify new, unseen data. Whether it's predicting house prices based on historical data or classifying emails as spam or not, supervised learning algorithms excel at tasks with clear labels and well-defined patterns.

Another type of machine learning algorithm is **unsupervised learning**, which intrigued me with its resemblance to the apprentice's exploration of the alchemist's library, filled with ancient scrolls waiting to be deciphered.

Unsupervised learning algorithms work with unlabeled data, seeking to discover hidden patterns or structures within the data itself. These algorithms cluster similar data points together or find meaningful representations of the data without any prior knowledge of the desired outcomes. Unsupervised learning opens the door to exploration and discovery, uncovering valuable insights that may have gone unnoticed.

I was particularly captivated by the concept of reinforcement learning, reminiscent of the apprentice's quest to master the alchemist's craft through trial and error. Reinforcement learning algorithms learn from interaction with an environment, receiving feedback in the form of rewards or penalties based on their actions. Through repeated iterations, these algorithms strive to maximize their cumulative rewards, adapting their strategies and decision-making processes along the way. From training autonomous agents to play complex games to optimizing resource allocation in dynamic environments, reinforcement learning holds the promise of intelligent decision-making in challenging scenarios.

Lastly, I encountered the fascinating world of semi-supervised learning, akin to the apprentice's journey of combining both the learned techniques and intuitive experimentation. In semi-supervised learning, algorithms leverage a mix of labeled and unlabeled data to improve their performance. By using the limited labeled data available alongside the vast amounts of unlabeled data, these algorithms can enhance their understanding and make more accurate predictions. Semi-supervised learning bridges the gap between the precision of supervised learning and the exploratory nature of unsupervised learning, offering a powerful approach for harnessing the potential of large, partially labeled datasets.

As I reflected on the diverse types of machine learning algorithms, I realized that each played a vital role in the alchemical process of turning raw data into meaningful insights. Whether it was following instructions in supervised learning, uncovering hidden patterns in unsupervised learning, exploring new possibilities in reinforcement learning, or blending knowledge in semi-supervised learning, these algorithms held the key to transforming data into valuable knowledge.

We have now journeyed through the alchemist's apprentice's exploration of different types of machine learning algorithms. We have witnessed the power and versatility of supervised learning, the curiosity-driven nature of unsupervised learning, the adaptive and experimental spirit of reinforcement learning, and the harmonious blend of labeled and unlabeled data in semi-supervised learning. As we move forward, let us continue to unlock the potential of these algorithms, combining art and science to unveil the hidden treasures within our data.

***

CHAPTER 5: THE DATA WHISPERER: UNVEILING THE SECRETS OF DATA PREPROCESSING

"Garbage in, garbage out." - George Fuechsel

As I delved deeper into the intricate world of machine learning, I stumbled upon a profound quote by George Fuechsel that resonated with my quest for knowledge. The quote reminded me of the crucial role that data plays in the success of any machine learning endeavor. Just as a skilled whisperer can calm even the wildest of beasts, a data whisperer possesses the power to tame and transform unruly data into a harmonious symphony of information.

In your own journey to becoming a data whisperer, you will discover that data preprocessing is the enchanted art that brings order and clarity to the chaotic realm of raw data. It is the vital process of transforming and preparing the data for analysis, ensuring that it is in a suitable format for the machine learning algorithms to work their magic.

Just like a skilled musician who carefully tunes each instrument before a performance, a data whisperer meticulously cleanses and prepares the data to remove noise, inconsistencies, and outliers. This ensures that the algorithms can focus on the essence of the data, extracting valuable patterns and insights. From handling missing values and correcting errors to standardizing and normalizing the data, each step in the data preprocessing journey contributes to the symphony of accurate and reliable results.

As you embark on your own data-whispering adventure, you will encounter various techniques that allow you to wield your transformative powers over the data. **Feature scaling**, for instance, acted as a musical conductor, harmonizing the different features of the dataset by bringing them to a similar scale. This prevented certain features from dominating the analysis due to their larger numerical values, ensuring a fair representation of all aspects of the data.

Another essential technique in your data whispering arsenal will be **feature encoding**, a process akin to translating languages for seamless communication. Categorical variables, such as colors or labels, were transformed into numerical representations, enabling the algorithms to comprehend and extract insights from them. Whether through one-hot encoding or label encoding, these techniques allow you to bridge the gap between the human-readable and machine-understandable worlds.

Data normalization, the virtuoso's touch, allows you to rescale the data to a standard range, removing any biases that may exist due to varying units or measurement scales. By bringing the data into a consistent and normalized form, you empower the algorithms to make fair comparisons and draw meaningful conclusions.

Yet, the journey of a data whisperer doesn't end with mere preprocessing. As I delved further, I discovered the enchanting realm of **feature engineering**. It is here that you truly harness your creative prowess, extracting new features from the existing ones, uncovering hidden relationships, and capturing domain knowledge in the process. Feature engineering breathed life into the data, imbuing it with the richness and depth necessary for the algorithms to unearth profound insights.

As we unravel the secrets of data preprocessing, we step into the shoes of the data whisperer, armed with the knowledge and techniques to transform raw data into a symphony of intelligence. Just as a skilled conductor can orchestrate a magnificent performance, we hold the power to unlock the full potential of our data, allowing the machine learning algorithms to perform their magical feats.

In the next chapter, we shall journey into the realm of model selection and evaluation, where we will witness the culmination of our efforts as we choose the most suitable algorithms and assess their performance. Together, let us continue on this wondrous path of discovery, guided by the spirit of the data whisperer and the power of data preprocessing.

***

CHAPTER 6: THE CREATIVE CANVAS: FEATURE ENGINEERING FOR EXCEPTIONAL ML MODELS

"Give me a lever long enough and a fulcrum on which to place it, and I shall move the world." - Archimedes

As I immersed myself deeper into the realm of machine learning, I stumbled upon a timeless quote by Archimedes that spoke volumes about the power of leverage. Little did I know that this quote would become the guiding principle in my exploration of feature engineering—an art that empowers us to create extraordinary machine learning models.

Imagine yourself as a painter, standing before a blank canvas, armed with a palette of colors and brushes of various sizes. You possess the vision to create a masterpiece, but it is the careful selection and skillful application of each brushstroke that brings your creation to life. Feature engineering, my dear reader, is your creative canvas, and the features you engineer are the brushstrokes that transform raw data into meaningful representations.

In this chapter, we shall embark on a journey that will unlock the true potential of your models through the art of feature engineering. Just as a master artist carefully selects and blends colors to evoke emotions and convey meaning, we shall select, transform, and combine the raw ingredients of data to capture the essence of the problem at hand.

Like an alchemist turning base metals into gold, feature engineering involves extracting, creating, and selecting features that possess the power to illuminate patterns and relationships within the data. It is the leverage that moves the world of machine learning, enabling us to reveal insights that would otherwise remain hidden.

One such technique in our feature engineering toolbox is **polynomial expansion**—a process that allows us to create higher-order features by raising existing features to different powers. This artistic stroke of mathematical brilliance enriches our models by capturing nonlinear relationships that may exist within the data, adding depth and complexity to our predictive capabilities.

Another technique that breathes life into our models is **feature interaction**. Just as different colors blend and interact to create new shades and hues, the interaction between features can unlock a wealth of information. By multiplying or dividing features or exploring their ratios, we can capture synergies and dependencies that hold the key to understanding the intricacies of our data.

But feature engineering is not limited to mere mathematical transformations. We also have the power to enrich our models with domain knowledge and human intuition! The inclusion of domain-specific features—those derived from our deep understanding of the problem at hand—infuses our models with a level of context and expertise that can set them apart. These features act as guideposts, leading our models to make more informed decisions and uncover nuanced insights.

However, like any artistic endeavor, feature engineering requires experimentation and refinement. Just as a painter steps back from their canvas to assess their work, we too must iterate, test, and fine-tune our feature engineering choices. It is through this iterative process that we discover the delicate balance between simplicity and complexity, ensuring that our models possess the right level of sophistication without sacrificing interpretability.

Dear reader, as we venture into the realm of feature engineering, let us embrace our inner artist and unleash our creativity. Armed with the Archimedean lever of feature engineering, we have the power to move the world of machine learning and craft models that transcend expectations.

In the next chapter, we shall embark on the next stage of our journey—the crystal ball. Together, let us continue on this artistic odyssey, driven by the passion to create exceptional machine learning models that inspire and transform.

***

CHAPTER 7: THE CRYSTAL BALL: PREDICTIVE MODELING AND FORECASTING MADE EASY

"Prediction is very difficult, especially if it's about the future." - Niels Bohr

As we delved deeper into the world of machine learning, we might stumble upon a quote by the renowned physicist Niels Bohr that perfectly encapsulated the challenges and allure of predictive modeling. The notion of peering into the future, armed with data and algorithms, has always fascinated humanity. We have an innate desire to understand what lies ahead, to anticipate the twists and turns of our journey, and to make informed decisions based on those insights.

Imagine, dear reader, if we had a crystal ball—a tool that could unlock the mysteries of the future. Predictive modeling, my dear friend, is our modern-day crystal ball, guiding us through the fog of uncertainty and illuminating the path forward. It is a powerful technique that harnesses the patterns and trends hidden within our data to forecast what is to come.

In this chapter, we embark on a captivating journey into the realm of predictive modeling, where we will demystify its principles and equip ourselves with the tools to make accurate predictions. Just as an expert fortune-teller deciphers the symbols and signs to reveal glimpses of destiny, we will learn how to transform raw data into actionable predictions.

At the heart of predictive modeling lies the art of feature selection. Like a skilled archaeologist sifting through layers of sediment, we carefully curate the features that hold the most predictive power. It is through this discerning process that we unearth the gems, the variables that contribute significantly to our predictive accuracy. By focusing on these essential features, we avoid the noise and distractions that can cloud our crystal ball.

Once we have assembled our arsenal of features, we embark on the grand quest of model selection. We explore a myriad of algorithms, each with its own strengths and weaknesses, seeking the one that aligns best with our data and objectives. Just as seasoned explorer selects the right tools and provisions for their journey, we choose the algorithm that will navigate us through the complexities of our predictive landscape.

But our journey does not end there, for predictive modeling is not merely a solitary endeavor. It is a dance between art and science, requiring constant refinement and fine-tuning. We validate our models using various evaluation metrics and techniques, ensuring that they possess the predictive prowess we seek. Like virtuoso musicians, we strive for harmony and precision, fine-tuning our models to strike the right chords of accuracy and generalization.

The power of predictive modeling extends far beyond the realm of fortune-telling. It finds application in diverse fields, from finance and healthcare to marketing and weather forecasting. It enables us to make data-driven decisions, anticipate market trends, optimize resources, and even save lives. The crystal ball of predictive modeling grants us a glimpse into what lies ahead, empowering us to act with foresight and confidence.

Now, as we embrace the realm of predictive modeling, let us harness its power responsibly and ethically. Let us recognize the limitations and uncertainties that accompany our predictions and use them as tools for informed decision-making. The crystal ball of predictive modeling is a marvelous gift—one that opens doors to new possibilities and transforms the way we navigate the complexities of our world.

In the next chapter, we delve into the realm of hidden patterns. Together, let us continue this enchanting journey, guided by the wisdom of Niels Bohr and driven by our insatiable curiosity to unravel the secrets of the future.

***

CHAPTER 8: THE HIDDEN PATTERNS: UNLEASHING THE POWER OF CLUSTERING AND PATTERN RECOGNITION

"Learn how to see. Realize that everything connects to everything else." - Leonardo da Vinci

As we delved deeper into the world of machine learning, the words of the brilliant Leonardo da Vinci echoed in our minds. Indeed, the world is filled with intricate connections and hidden patterns waiting to be discovered. Just as Leonardo unraveled the secrets of nature and art, we too can unlock the power of clustering and pattern recognition to reveal the hidden gems within our data.

In this captivating chapter, we embark on a journey of exploration, peering into the depths of our datasets in search of meaningful patterns and connections. Like a skilled detectives, we will don our investigative hats and uncover the mysteries that lie beneath the surface.

Clustering, my dear AI explorer, is the art of grouping similar data points together as if we were placing them in the same category based on their inherent characteristics. Just as a curator organizes a vast collection of artifacts into cohesive exhibits, we strive to find order amidst the chaos of our data. Through clustering, we gain insights into the natural divisions and relationships that exist within our datasets.

But how do we recognize these patterns? How do we discern the threads that bind seemingly disparate elements together? Pattern recognition, my friend, is the key. It is the ability to identify recurring structures, motifs, and behaviors within our data. Like seasoned musician who recognizes familiar melodies, we train our algorithms to detect the underlying patterns that define our datasets.

Imagine, for a moment, you are walking through an art gallery filled with abstract paintings. At first glance, the paintings may appear random and chaotic, but as you look closer, you begin to see common shapes, colors, and themes that connect them. Clustering and pattern recognition allows us to create a similar experience with our data, revealing the hidden order that lies beneath the surface.

In the realm of business, clustering and pattern recognition offer a treasure trove of possibilities. They empower us to segment our customers into distinct groups, enabling targeted marketing campaigns and personalized experiences. They help us identify anomalies and fraud within financial transactions, safeguarding our resources. They even assist in medical diagnostics, aiding in the early detection of diseases by recognizing subtle patterns within patient data.

As we dive into the world of clustering and pattern recognition, let us embrace the spirit of curiosity and exploration. Let us look beyond the surface and seek out the connections that weave our data together. In doing so, we unlock a world of possibilities, where hidden insights and valuable knowledge await our discovery.

In the next chapter, we venture into the realm of natural language processing, where we unravel the intricacies of human language and harness its power to understand, interpret, and generate text. Together, let us continue this awe-inspiring journey, guided by the wisdom of Leonardo da Vinci and driven by our insatiable desire to uncover the hidden patterns that shape our world.

***

CHAPTER 9: THE TALKING MACHINES: AN INTRODUCTION TO NATURAL LANGUAGE PROCESSING

"Language is the dress of thought."
- Samuel Johnson

As we ventured even further into the realm of artificial intelligence, we became fascinated by the wondrous world of **Natural Language Processing (NLP)**. Samuel Johnson's words echoed in my mind, reminding me of the profound connection between language and our thoughts. Just as our words shape our understanding of the world, NLP enables machines to comprehend and interact with human language.

In this captivating chapter, we embark on a journey that unravels the mysteries of NLP, where machines learn to understand, interpret, and communicate with us through the power of language. It is a realm where words come alive, where machines become adept at deciphering the nuances of human communication.

Imagine, if you will, a machine that can read and comprehend a vast library of texts, extracting meaning and knowledge from its pages. Just like a wise scholar poring over ancient manuscripts, our NLP models delve deep into the intricacies of language, recognizing the subtleties of grammar, syntax, and semantics. They unravel the threads of meaning woven into every sentence, unlocking a treasure trove of information that can shape our understanding of the world.

But NLP is not limited to mere understanding. It extends its grasp into the realm of human-like communication. Picture a machine that can converse with us, responding to our queries, understanding our intentions, and even generating human-like text. It is a realm where machines become our language companions, engaging in meaningful conversations that blur the lines between human and artificial intelligence.

NLP finds applications in countless domains, transforming industries and enhancing our daily lives. In healthcare, it aids in analyzing medical records, extracting vital information, and assisting in diagnoses. In customer service, it powers chatbots that provide instant support and personalized assistance. In finance, it analyzes vast volumes of text data to uncover trends and sentiments, enabling informed decision-making.

In our personal lives, NLP is the technology behind virtual assistants that listen to our voice commands, translate languages in real time, and even generate personalized recommendations for our entertainment and shopping needs. It is a testament to the power of language and the incredible potential of machines to understand and engage with us on a deeply human level.

As we delve into the world of NLP, let us marvel at the vastness and complexity of human language. Let us embrace the opportunities it presents, as well as the challenges it poses. Together, we will unlock the secrets of linguistic understanding and embark on a journey where machines become fluent in the art of communication.

In the next chapter, we will explore the fascinating world of intelligent vision. Let's continue this extraordinary expedition into the heart of artificial intelligence, inspired by the words of Samuel Johnson and driven by our insatiable quest for knowledge and understanding.

***

CHAPTER 10: THE INTELLIGENT VISION: DELVING INTO COMPUTER VISION AND IMAGE RECOGNITION

"Every image is a story waiting to be told."

Chris Orwig's profound words remind me of the countless stories embedded within each image, waiting to be unraveled by the keen eyes of intelligent machines. To be honest I was captivated by the extraordinary power of computer vision and image recognition.

In this enthralling chapter, we venture into the realm of **computer vision**, where machines learn to perceive, interpret, and make sense of the visual world that surrounds us. Just like an artist who can transform a blank canvas into a masterpiece, computer vision empowers machines to understand the intricate details and narratives hidden within images.

Imagine, for a moment, a machine that can see and comprehend the contents of a photograph. It perceives the shapes, colors, and textures, and can even recognize and identify the objects within the scene. It is as if a veil is lifted, revealing a world where pixels come to life and images speak their stories.

Computer vision encompasses a vast array of applications, revolutionizing industries and reshaping our daily lives. In healthcare, it aids in medical imaging analysis, helping doctors detect diseases and anomalies with greater accuracy. In autonomous vehicles, it enables machines to navigate and interpret their surroundings, ensuring safe and efficient transportation. In retail, it powers the visual search and recommendation systems, assisting shoppers in finding products that align with their preferences.

But computer vision goes beyond mere perception.

It unlocks the power of image recognition, where machines not only see but also understand the content of images. They can classify objects, recognize faces, and even interpret emotions displayed on human faces. It is a world where machines become visual storytellers, decoding the narratives woven within the pixels and providing us with valuable insights and information.

In our personal lives, computer vision has become an integral part of our daily experiences. We capture cherished moments through our smartphones, and AI algorithms automatically organize and tag our photos based on the content they contain. We effortlessly unlock our devices using facial recognition technology, and virtual reality transports us to immersive visual realms that ignite our imagination.

As you delve deeper into the realm of computer vision and image recognition, let you appreciate the remarkable progress made in understanding and interpreting visual information. Let you marvel at the machines' ability to perceive the world through our eyes and decipher the stories embedded within each image.

In the next chapter, we will venture into the realm

of ethical challenges in ML. We will continue this extraordinary journey into the realm of artificial intelligence, guided by the words of Chris Orwig and driven by our insatiable curiosity to uncover its secrets.

***

CHAPTER 11: THE ETHICAL COMPASS: NAVIGATING THE ETHICAL CHALLENGES IN ML

"Ethics is knowing the difference between what you have a right to do and what is right to do." - Potter Stewart

As our journey through the realm of artificial intelligence continues, we find ourselves standing at a critical crossroad: the intersection of technology and ethics. This reminds me of the crucial importance of navigating the ethical challenges that arise in the world of machine learning.

In this chapter, we embark on a profound exploration of the ethical implications surrounding the use and development of machine learning algorithms. As we push the boundaries of what is possible with AI, it becomes paramount to pause and reflect on the impact our creations have on individuals, society, and the world at large.

Consider, for a moment, the immense power bestowed upon intelligent machines. They possess the ability to analyze vast amounts of data, make decisions, and even shape human behavior. With such capabilities, it is essential to ensure that the ethical compass guides their actions and decisions.

One of the key ethical concerns in machine learning revolves around **biases** and **fairness**. As machines learn from data, they can inadvertently inherit the biases present in the data, perpetuating social inequalities and discrimination.

For instance, if a facial recognition algorithm is trained primarily on a specific demographic, it may struggle to accurately identify individuals from underrepresented groups. As responsible stewards of this technology, it is our duty to mitigate biases and strive for fairness, ensuring that our algorithms treat all individuals equitably.

Privacy is another ethical consideration that demands our attention. Machine learning algorithms rely on vast amounts of personal data to make accurate predictions and decisions. However, this data can be sensitive and vulnerable to misuse. We must prioritize the protection of individuals' privacy rights, implementing robust security measures and transparent data practices that respect the sanctity of personal information.

Transparency and explainability also play a crucial role in the ethical use of machine learning. As algorithms make decisions that impact individuals' lives, it is vital to provide clear explanations and justifications for those decisions. This allows users to understand the reasoning behind the algorithm's choices and holds developers accountable for the outcomes generated by their creations.

Furthermore, the ethical considerations extend beyond technical aspects to encompass broader societal impacts. Automation driven by AI technologies has the potential to disrupt industries and reshape the workforce, leading to job displacements and economic disparities. It is imperative to proactively address these challenges by fostering reskilling and upskilling initiatives, ensuring a smooth transition and inclusivity in the face of technological advancements.

In navigating the ethical challenges of machine learning, we must adopt a multidisciplinary approach. Collaboration between technologists, ethicists, policymakers, and stakeholders from diverse backgrounds is essential in shaping responsible AI practices and policies. By engaging in open dialogue and collective decision-making, we can foster an environment where the benefits of machine learning are maximized while minimizing the risks and unintended consequences.

As we move forward on this journey, let us hold steadfast to our ethical compass, making conscious choices that align with our moral principles and societal values. By embracing the responsibility of ethical decision-making, we can ensure that the tremendous potential of machine learning is harnessed for the greater good of humanity.

In the last chapter, we will explore the future of AI, where machines and humans collaborate to create a new era of possibilities.

***

CHAPTER 12: THE FUTURE UNVEILED: EXPLORING CUTTING-EDGE ML APPLICATIONS

"The best way to predict the future is
to create it." - Peter Drucker

The possibilities that lie ahead in the realm of machine learning are as vast as the universe itself. In this chapter, we embark on a thrilling journey into the world of cutting-edge ML applications, where innovation and imagination converge to shape the future.

Imagine a world where medical diagnoses are made with unprecedented accuracy, saving countless lives. Picture self-driving cars navigating our roads, reducing accidents and congestion. Envision personalized recommendations that anticipate our needs and desires, making every interaction seamless and delightful. These are just a few glimpses of the incredible potential that lies within the realm of cutting-edge ML applications.

One area where ML is revolutionizing the landscape in **healthcare**. The ability of intelligent algorithms to analyze vast amounts of medical data and identify patterns holds immense promise for early disease detection, personalized treatment plans, and drug discovery. From detecting anomalies in medical images to predicting patient outcomes, ML is transforming healthcare into a proactive, precise, and patient-centric field.

Transportation is another domain where ML is reshaping the future. Autonomous vehicles powered by ML algorithms are paving the way for safer, more efficient, and environmentally friendly transportation systems. These vehicles learn from their surroundings, adapt to changing conditions, and make split-second decisions to ensure the well-being of passengers and pedestrians alike. The future of transportation is on the horizon, and it's filled with innovation and possibilities.

In the realm of **e-commerce** and entertainment, ML applications are personalizing our experiences like never before. Sophisticated recommendation systems analyze our preferences, browsing history, and behavior to curate personalized suggestions that captivate and engage us. From personalized movie recommendations to tailored product suggestions, ML algorithms are transforming how we discover and engage with the world around us.

Beyond these specific domains, ML is permeating every aspect of our lives. From virtual assistants that understand and respond to our voice commands to fraud detection systems that safeguard our financial transactions, the applications are as diverse as our imaginations. ML is the driving force behind the intelligent systems that empower us, augment our capabilities, and shape the way we interact with technology.

However, as we step into this future, it is essential to reflect on the ethical and societal implications of these cutting-edge applications. We must ensure that the benefits of ML are accessible to all, mitigate biases, and address concerns surrounding privacy, security, and accountability. By approaching these advancements with responsibility and a keen awareness of their potential impact, we can create a future that is not only technologically advanced but also human-centric.

The future unveiled before us is both exciting and humbling. It is a testament to human ingenuity, innovation, and our relentless pursuit of progress. As we harness the power of cutting-edge ML applications, let us remember the words of Peter Drucker: the future is ours to shape.

By nurturing our imagination, fostering collaboration, and embracing ethical practices, we can create a future that enriches our lives, empowers individuals and communities, and drives us toward a better tomorrow.

As our journey through the world of machine learning comes almost to an end, I am filled with gratitude for the opportunity to explore this captivating domain with you. We have delved into its intricacies, demystified its concepts, and witnessed the transformative power it holds.

The world of ML is ever-evolving, and as you continue on your own path, remember that the future is yours to create. Embrace the possibilities, unleash your imagination, and let the magic of machine learning guide you toward a future limited only by the boundaries of your dreams.

***

FINAL THOUGHTS

"A baby learns to crawl, walk and then run.
We are in the crawling stage when it comes to
applying machine learning." - Dave Waters

As we reach almost the end of this journey through the captivating world of machine learning, we find ourselves standing on the precipice of an extraordinary future. We have witnessed the incredible power of algorithms that can decipher hidden patterns in data, predict outcomes with astonishing accuracy, and unlock new frontiers of innovation. Machine learning has transcended its origins as a technological concept and has become an integral part of our lives, reshaping industries, revolutionizing the way we live and work, and offering limitless possibilities for the future.

Throughout this book, we have unraveled the mysteries of machine learning, guiding you through its core principles, exploring its diverse algorithms, and showcasing its practical applications. We have dived into the realms of predictive modeling, natural language processing, computer vision, and more, witnessing firsthand how these powerful tools are transforming industries such as healthcare, finance, transportation, and entertainment. We have navigated the ethical challenges and societal implications, reflecting on the responsibilities and considerations that come hand in hand with the rapid advancement of intelligent machines.

But beyond the technical intricacies, what makes machine learning truly remarkable is its potential to shape a future that is more efficient, more personalized, and more human-centric. The impact of machine learning extends far beyond the confines of algorithms and datasets. It touches the very essence of our society, our economy, and our collective progress. From enabling breakthroughs in medical diagnostics and personalized medicine to revolutionizing the way we interact with technology through voice assistants and chatbots, machine learning has become the driving force behind innovation and change.

In the coming years, we will witness an even greater integration of machine learning into our daily lives. The boundaries between humans and machines will continue to blur as intelligent systems become more adept at understanding and responding to our needs. The future holds the promise of autonomous vehicles navigating our roads, personalized virtual assistants anticipating our desires, and customized healthcare solutions tailored to our genetic makeup. Machine learning will empower us to unlock new frontiers, solve complex problems, and navigate the challenges that lie ahead.

However, as we embrace the immense potential of machine learning, we must remain vigilant and mindful of the ethical considerations that accompany this technological revolution. We must ensure that the power of machine learning is harnessed for the greater good, promoting transparency, fairness, and accountability. The responsibility lies not only with the researchers and engineers developing these technologies but also with the policymakers, organizations, and individuals who shape their applications and deployment.

In closing, we find ourselves at a crucial juncture in human history. The journey we have embarked upon through this book has revealed the extraordinary capabilities of machine learning and its profound impact on our lives. We stand on the threshold of a future where the boundaries of what is possible continue to expand, where intelligent machines work alongside us to tackle the greatest challenges of our time. As we navigate this ever-evolving landscape, let us remember the words of Andrew Ng:

Artificial intelligence is the new electricity.

Just as electricity transformed the world, AI and machine learning have the power to ignite a new era of innovation and progress.

So, let us embrace the possibilities, harness the power of machine learning, and shape a future that is not only intelligent but also compassionate, equitable, and sustainable. As we continue to explore the frontiers of technology, may we do so with a deep understanding of its potential and a steadfast commitment to using it for the betterment of humanity.

Thank you for joining me on this enlightening journey. May your endeavors in the realm of machine learning be filled with curiosity, creativity, and a profound sense of purpose. The future awaits, and together, we can unlock its limitless potential with the power of machine learning.

***

THE POWER OF YOUR REVIEW

Your feedback matters! If you found this book valuable, please leave a review on Amazon.

https://www.amazon.com/dp/B0C8ZN1CGK

Your review provides valuable insights for me and helps other readers discover this book.

EXPAND YOUR
AI JOURNEY

If you enjoyed this book, you may also be interested in exploring other books written by me. Visit my author page on Amazon:

https://www.amazon.com/author/kuznietsov_ivan

Discover more captivating reads on the intersection of technology and human potential!

ACKNOWLEDGMENTS

I would like to express my deepest gratitude to all the individuals who have contributed to the creation of this book.

First and foremost, I am thankful to my family for their unwavering support and encouragement throughout this journey.

I am also indebted to my friends and colleagues who provided valuable insights and feedback.

Additionally, I extend my appreciation to the editors, designers, and publishing team who played an integral role in shaping this work.

Last but not least, I am grateful to your, dear reader, whose curiosity and passion for knowledge continue to inspire me. Your support is truly invaluable.

BIBLIOGRAPHY

Books:

1. Hastie, Trevor, Robert Tibshirani, and Jerome Friedman. "The Elements of Statistical Learning: Data Mining, Inference, and Prediction." Springer, 2009.
2. Goodfellow, Ian, Yoshua Bengio, and Aaron Courville. "Deep Learning." MIT Press, 2016.
3. Chollet, François. "Deep Learning with Python." Manning Publications, 2017.

Research Papers and Journals:

1. LeCun, Yann, et al. "Gradient-based learning applied to document recognition." Proceedings of the IEEE 86.11 (1998): 2278-2324.
2. Krizhevsky, Alex, Ilya Sutskever, and Geoffrey E. Hinton. "ImageNet classification with deep convolutional neural networks." Advances in neural information processing systems. 2012.

3. Sutskever, Ilya, Oriol Vinyals, and Quoc V. Le. "Sequence to sequence learning with neural networks." Advances in neural information processing systems. 2014.
4. Vaswani, Ashish, et al. "Attention is all you need." Advances in neural information processing systems. 2017.